Insights

FROM THE OTHER SIDE
OF THE COUCH

DAVRIELLE J.
VALLEY, NCC , MS , CT

Preface

This book is not a novel. It is not meant to be a page-turner, but instead, thought-provoking. The most challenging thing a human can do is reflect. Reflect on themselves and the relationships they have with others.

For every page,

Stop, think, and *REFLECT*.

A counselor is a giver. A giver of time.
A giver of knowledge. A giver of self.

It takes a lot for one person to create a safe
space for another to just be.
It is within these times that even
we gain insights.

Contents

Transgenerational Trauma

Healing begins at home...

Trauma is subjective. Never let anyone belittle your experience or its impact on your life, especially if they played a role in it.

Be open to returning home; it is
where your healing lies.

When you get lost and forget who you are,
it is time to return home.

Returning home does not mean physically
going back to your childhood home. It means
reflecting and working to heal the wounds of
our youth.

For it is in this healing that we rediscover our
true selves.

You stay in that toxic relationship for so long because the hurt feels familiar to the pain of your unresolved parental trauma.

Family secrets are the vehicle that transmits trauma from one generation to another.

There was much self-doubt in me. I realized it came from never learning to trust my voice. Whether being told I could not achieve or protected from making particular decisions, the only message I received was that I did not know what was good for me.

Avoiding familial patterns does not resolve them; it only repeats them.

Your emotional growth may trigger
the emotional immaturity of those around you.

The stories others have of you are through the lens of their experiences and maybe even their insecurities. It is admirable to reflect on their perspective and weigh if there is any truth. However, never buy what they are selling wholesale. Their views do not define you.

A parentified child will only turn into an over-functioning adult.

To ease our anxiety, we *over-function* and do for others what they can do for themselves. Only to now be caught in the trap of them now *under-functioning*. A never-ending cycle unless we learn to manage our anxieties and allow others to function up!

You may have experienced trauma, but those experiences are what you *lived* through. They are not who you are.

Providing only your basic needs may be your parents' way to show affection. This type of love may be all they received and the only way they know how to demonstrate love. Remember, your longing for a deeper connection is valid even if they do not understand it.

I have been guilty of viewing one parent
through the eyes of another. That was not my
experience to own.

There were times, I did not have the mindset to receive the wisdom of others, and I had to learn the painful way that they were right.

We create a caricature of our parents in our minds as children. The 'perfect parent' that we expect them to be.

As we get older, we realize the person we created is rarely ever who they are.

Allow yourself to grieve the parent you always needed but never had.

Greater understanding quenches hate.

Good intentions of a parent can scar you in ways you cannot verbalize until adulthood.

I have made bad decisions that I have no one to blame but myself.

It may be easier to say, "I am this way because of my parents."

The truth is, it is much harder to admit, "And I remain this way because of me."

We have fled the abuse of our childhood homes only to continue emotionally abusing ourselves.

We all carry baggage. Some of us know what is in our suitcases and have been working on unpacking. In contrast, some refuse to open the bag altogether.

When you unpack, you gain skills and strength to overcome other obstacles. This power is resilience.

The decisions you make today will either transfer your trauma or your resilience.

A child's first love is often its parent, and a broken heart finds many of us early.

If stuck in our survival mode, we are not living because we are not truly present. Now we must switch our mindset from surviving to thriving.

One day at a time, Choosing to be present, Choosing to be consistent, Choosing to be mindful.

You are a revolutionary. You are breaking the chains of generational trauma and advocating for your betterment, ultimately creating healthier patterns of love, authenticity, and connection for yourself and your future.

This revolution is the making of a true hero.

I face my demons head-on so that they do not face my children.

Healing

Healing sometimes hurts...

You are changing. You are different.
You try to explain it, but words cannot describe
the process. You are going through
your metamorphosis.

Not everyone in your life is going to understand
your journey.

It is *your* journey.

The one place people run from the most is their minds. Your mind can trap you or liberate you, but it all depends on the environment you create.

Plant positive seeds of love, faith, and hope, and be careful to water them less they wilt.

There is more bravery in sitting with your feelings than not feeling anything at all.

If no one has told you, then I will.

You are stronger than you think.

Your needs are essential, and your feelings are valid.

A turtle carries the weight of its shell every day. Yet, when scared, it looks within for strength and protection. We, too, should learn to look inward to gain power and strength from our burdens.

Every day is going to be different. Some days it will be easier to stay positive.

Others may feel numb. Then there will be those days where all you can do is feel. Feel everything.

It does not matter which day it is. Remember to be gentle with yourself. That is how you do your best.

For too long have I believed that I am not worthy of love. I give it freely, but my heart has been closed to accept it.

A reminder to myself: I am both a *giver* and a *receiver* of love.

Every layer of pain that they peeled off added a new level of torment. Still, they showed up and continued the work.

Turning jealousy into admiration can save your heart from bitterness and open your mind to ways of improving.

Caution: The pain of healing can be so overwhelming that we may long to return to what hurt us, at least that pain was familiar.

You *feel* broken, but you are not.

How we feel can often be so heavy that we begin to believe it is *who* we are. You are not your feelings. You are what you do with them.

People *can* change. I see it every day. If only they want it bad enough. If only they recognize their power. If only they become aware of how they hurt others when they do not.

The positive feeling does not always come first.
Sometimes you have to *believe* first.

I had to validate my voice first before I could learn to validate the voices of others.

It would be freeing if we could release that which brings us pain. Yet, when pain is familiar, letting go is difficult because we do not know what follows.

The process of healing is like giving birth. It is messy and painful, but when you get past it, you would happily do it again for the result that it bears.

Comparing your suffering to another will only invalidate both experiences. Your experiences are your own. Others may have similar trauma, but the way you experience it is uniquely yours.

Name the demons (anxiety, depression, etc.). It
will remind your brain that they are not you.

It had snuffed out your light. The darkness consumed you. However, you could never stay in that place forever.

A spark reignited, small at first, a little hope in who you could be. Since then, it has been a fight to protect that light.

There is a fear of letting it grow because it would draw others, and what if they were to diminish it again?

Still, there is faith in you that you will find people who will help you protect it, those that will enhance it.

You can be vulnerable and still strong.

True liberation comes from recognizing that you hold the key.

Many people's reactions are not about you; it is about them. It is only personal if you make it, and then it is not about them but you.

Relationships

No man is an island...

When people do not appreciate your process, let that motivate you to show them your progress.

Sometimes the people who walk out of your life think that your light will go with them. Do yourself a favor and shine brighter.

We attract relationships that mirror what we think we are worth.

Consumed with ensuring everyone around me likes me that I never stopped to ask myself if I liked them.

For the sake of the peace, I have often been the martyr.

Creating an attachment over trauma can form a bond so strong it can be mistaken for love.

Of others, ask yourself, "Who are you when I have nothing to give?"

If the physical attraction and fear of loneliness were not so strong, would you even choose this person as a friend?

Instead of looking for a relationship to 'complete' you, finding one that will create an environment safe to grow and evolve may bring greater liberation.

Repeated negative behaviors, despite
your protest, are no longer a mistake. It is a
pattern.

Everyone is flawed. You do need to be perfect to be loved. Neither should you require perfection to love another. Love inspires each other towards progress, not perfection.

We love, yet only how we know, which may not be the way it is needed.

People cannot read minds; that is the reason
we have a voice.

Not always have I been a good listener. There were times I made their issues about me and left them alone in their discomfort.

There is a vast difference between unity and co-dependence.

Co-dependence says, "I cannot live without you. You must *become* me."

Unity says, "I love who you are. Let us join together."

One consumes while the other respects the role played in the greater whole.

Your expectations are your own.

Find your circle with people who accept you, motivate you, cheer for you, and sit with you. These are the ingredients needed to bloom. It is the magic of connection.

You cannot slay someone else's dragons.

When we experience hurt from unhealthy connections, we may feel justified in terminating all relationships with others. However, by forming this detachment, we rob ourselves of the most genuine gift humanity offers, to be fully known and accepted by another.

You deserve connections that nourish the person you are becoming, not triggering the version you are outgrowing.

Be curious, not critical.

It is a lot easier to communicate through the lens of a judge. Quick with a verdict of "guilty" or "not guilty." A real challenge is to take the position of wanting to understand another.

The road less traveled is the road where true connection lies.

Do not let your boundaries become barriers.

I had moments when the toxic person in the situation was me. I have taken accountability for those actions. Daily, I work towards becoming a better version of myself. Still, it is a heavyweight to acknowledge the responsibility of inflicting pain on another.

First, I had to forgive myself for being able to hurt someone for whom I cared. Then, I had to have the courage to ask for that person's forgiveness. Lastly, I recognized that I was at their mercy and had no control over how they received my pardon.

The last was the most difficult to accept.

Love brings clarity, not confusion.

You can care about someone without taking responsibility for their problems.

A wound-mate reignites your triggers. A help-mate respects your triggers, helps you identify them, and invests in your healing.

When it comes to romantic partners, we often form our physical 'type' through the lens of our insecurities.

Be more vocal without hostility.

We may not always know what to say when someone we care about is hurting. What we can do is be present. Sit with them in their pain. We do not have to try to fix their problems because their pain makes *us* feel uncomfortable. It is more than enough to provide the space they need to be vulnerable.

People are only perfect in Disney movies. Humans are flawed, and it takes time, consistency, and patience to make relationships work.

Chemistry is passion. Compatibility is fit.

Passion wanes with time. Fit can become a foundation upon which to build.

Love is bottomless. It expands and changes as we allow ourselves and the other person to grow. Loving always who they currently are, not who they used to be, or who we want them to become.

Become the right person instead of looking for the right person.

Switch from looking to becoming.

A relationship to heal together, A friend to discover the world,

A partner with whom to build a dream.

Lust is blind; infatuation is blind, but Love is not blind.

Love sees everything with both eyes wide open. It encompasses the passion of lust and the hopefulness of infatuation, yet it dives much deeper. It sees the person for exactly who they are, who they were in the past, and who they could be in the future. And not only does it see, but it accepts, completely without judgment.

Love is not afraid to speak its mind because love corrects and feels liberated, knowing that it will never leave. Only Love is vulnerable, completely naked. Lust and infatuation can only attain physical nakedness, but love gives even more and is bare mentally, emotionally, and spiritually.

Love would never willingly harm; instead, it seeks to protect because it is like loving yourself when you love. So you can only truly love someone else after you have learned first to love yourself.

Do not let the length of a relationship or friendship blind you to toxic tendencies.

Blood makes you related. Loyalty makes you family, and family shows up.

There is an expectation that if others did not understand us, we did not communicate correctly.

Sadly, you can use the right tone, be politically correct and send as coherent a message as possible, and still, it does not guarantee that the person is open to receiving it.

Know that you have done your part. You made the call, but they did not pick up. Maybe it is simply not their time to receive the message.

Expectations of people will bring disappointment. Expectations of Christ will bring unmeasurable blessings.

If you cannot be yourself with them, then they are not your people.

Better to lose friends than lose yourself.

Some persons fall in love with the idea of love.
Then the fairy tale often turns into a nightmare
where the prince remains a beast.

Moving on does not mean rushing into another relationship. It means taking the time to heal and put yourself back together.

Otherwise, you may find yourself tracking the mud of your past relationship onto the shiny floors of your new one. Remember, messy floors can be challenging to hide.

If their only consistent trait is being inconsistent, there is a problem!

People, like thoughts, come and go in your life. You have the power to choose which you entertain.

Before requiring accountability, I must first hold myself accountable.

I have learned that not everyone should have access to my energy.

I have mistaken attention for love. It was a dangerous mistake to make.

A good friend can leave their world of sunshine to climb down into your darkness to sit with you.

True love is so profound that it can withstand the test of time. You have to be patient enough to find it and wise enough to look straight at it.

Selfull

*The ability to give of oneself
without losing oneself*

If you viewed yourself through the eyes of your Creator, you would love you too.

A lack of self-love is the highest form of abandonment.

Arrogance puffs up, but self-awareness brings humility in knowing there are always things left to be improved.

People will tell you what you are worth if you do not know it, and you may not like the price tag.

Self-growth is not a journey for the faint-hearted. For it is a journey, limited only by our vulnerability, that lasts for a lifetime.

Being kind to yourself only when you feel good
is like taking medicine when you are healthy.

P.S.A. - Not everyone is going to like you...And that is okay.

Visualization. Verbalization. Manifestation.

See it. Speak it. Be it.

Picture the type of person you want to become. How do you carry yourself? How would your relationships look?

Affirm that image daily.

Each day, walk like it and talk like it. Become the change you want to see.

Adulthood is like childhood with responsibilities.

If you only reward a child when they do what you want, they may believe that you only love them transactionally. It is the same with self-love. If you only treat yourself kindly when you feel good, that's transactional love, not unconditional love.

Self-care involves more than taking care of yourself for the moment. It is about investing in yourself for the long run.

Some people thrive off of triggering reactions (fire) from us. Emotions fuel reactions that make them impulsive. You know the saying of going, "0 to 100 real quick". It is the strike of a match, where you do not think and say things you do not mean. Fire and fire only make a more explosive flame (conflict). The only way to put out a fire is to add water.

Responding (water) to the flame of others changes the entire dynamic of the issue. A calm tone, a thoughtful reply, even taking some space to think all work to deescalate the situation. It brings healing, resolve, and a chance for greater understanding.

Reacting is impulsive (fire). Responding is thoughtful (water).

Fall in love with discovering the unchartered territory of your mind.

Permanent decisions are better not made based on temporary feelings.

Empathy is a superpower that not all humans possess. It can be mistaken for weakness if the hero does not know how to contain it.

Being an emotionally mature adult means having the ability to adapt when there is no structure.

Be brave. Be kind.
Speak the truth with love.

The practice of self-love is not selfish but selfull. To be selfull means to give of oneself without losing oneself. It is about filling your cup to then pour into others.

The bravest thing you can do is, be yourself.

Never dim your inner light for the sake of someone else's ego.

You are there for everyone else. Wearing the superhero cape can be heavy on your shoulders. Wearing a mask for so long, you may have forgotten your true identity. It is all exhausting.

To show up as the best version of yourself, you have to take time to invest in yourself. Take off the cape, remove the mask. Save yourself first.

The world will not stop.

True self-love is not vanity—insecurity fuels vanity, not self-love.

There were many mountains I did not think I could climb over. The scars remain on my hands from the journey. Now, as I see this place I have never been before, there is a lightness, a freedom in my heart that makes it all worth it.

Self-love comes from vulnerability and authenticity with yourself, your complete self. Who you were, who you are, and whom you are becoming.

We must always be *doing* to be productive. That was the teaching. We learned to *do* rather than to *be*. We avoided stillness and burnt ourselves out. Remind yourself that rest can also be productive.

I have learned that saying 'no' is a power that
only the mentally strong can wield correctly.

I am like this for a purpose. I will never fulfill my purpose by trying to be someone else.

A war with self has no victors.

Constantly, we fight against ourselves, yet we want peace. Until we can put down our guns (negative self-talk and unhealthy behaviors), we will continue to die on the battlefield.

Realize that this is not a war to be won but a mission of self-rescue.

As I learn to love myself,
I am learning to love you.

Acknowledgments

As the subheading in the third section noted, "No man is an island." It is only through the love and support of those around me that I created this book. Many have impacted my life, thus this book; my grandmothers, aunts, uncles, cousins, teachers, pastors, and friends who have turned into family. All of you have believed in me and invested in my light, making this dream become a reality.

First, I must begin with my Creator, my Lord, and Savior, Jesus Christ. Only by God's grace do I exist and do what I love, serving others. His love has helped me learn to love myself in ways I have never imagined. It inspired me to share it with others in the only way I can, to write.

To my parents Avril and Derek: Your sacrifices never go unnoticed by me. The determination and perseverance I embody are inherited from you and ingrained in me as a way of life. I am grateful that you are my parents. You both are what I needed for this journey. There will never be a time I will not need you in my life.

Acknowledgments

To Yoel, Mekeila, Princess, Terri, Steph, and the rest of my friend family: Thank you for always loving me for who I am. Thank you for being my confidants when I needed someone to listen. Your encouragement made me brave enough to introduce myself to the world.

To my clients: Every one of you has left your mark on me. Every journey that we have embarked on together has paved new ground for my personal growth. I believe each person that crossed my path was by divine intervention.

This book would be non-existent without each one of you.

To the readers: Thank you for being open-minded to my thoughts and *insights.*

About the Author

Davrielle J. Valley is a National Certified Counselor, Clinical Traumatologist, and Family Therapist. She is also the founder of Evolvinu LLC, an Online Therapy Practice. Davrielle, affectionately known by her clients as DJ, has been practicing with clients for over 6 years. She has made it her mission to work with people who consider themselves fellow *GIVERS*. Connect with her on Instagram @ evolvin_u and Facebook @Evolvinu. For more information, search the link below.

www.evolvinu.com

Glossary

Accountability: the ability to hold oneself responsible for one's own decisions and actions

Authenticity: the quality of being genuine or real

Attachment: the psychological and emotional bond formed between two people

Boundary: limits that mark the area of comfort when interacting with others

Caricature: an image of a person that exaggerates particular characteristics

Chemistry: complex physical and emotional attraction between people

Co-dependence: excessive emotional and psychological reliance on a partner

Compatibility: the ability for two people to function together without conflict; a feeling of friendship and companionship

Connection: a deep emotional link between two people based on their level of vulnerability

Empathy: the ability to sense the emotions of another and imagine what they may be experiencing

Energy: the strength and fortitude needed to maintain physical and mental well-being; the positive or negative atmosphere created by a person

Evolve: to gradually transform into a better or more advanced state of being

Expectations: a strong belief that someone will or should behave in a particular way

Giver: someone who invests, nurtures, and pours into someone else

Help-mate: a partner in a relationship that creates an emotionally safe environment for healing and growth

Insecurities: aspects of a person that make them feel anxious or lack confidence

Manifestation: an action that shows or embodies something abstract

Metamorphosis: a process of change in the nature of a person

Over-function: to ease your anxiety by doing for others what they can do for themselves and therefore encouraging them to not function to their highest ability

Parentified: being forced into a parental role

Present: the ability to be conscious of what is happening around you and in you both physically and emotionally

Reacting: an impulsive retaliation driven by emotion

Responding: a purposeful, well-thought-out decision with the ability to stop, reflect, and adjust

Selfull: the ability to give of oneself without losing oneself

Toxic: gradual and subtly harmful or unpleasant effects; poisonous

Transactional: doing something in exchange for something in return

Transgenerational: transferring across multiple generations

Trauma: the distress caused by a real or perceived threat

Trigger: to elicit an automatic unfavorable emotional reaction

Under-functioning: to ease anxiety by allowing others to do for you what you can do for yourself

Unity: the state of more than one thing coming together to form a harmonious whole

Vanity: excessive pride or admiration for one's appearance or achievements

Verbalization: to express in words

Visualization: the creation of a mental image of something

Vulnerable: the potential to be open and authentic with both self and others

Wound-mate: an attachment with a partner that is formed based on trauma or the bond of a partner that inflicts pain on the other